How D

Important Questions
in Every Girl's Life

Susan Lutz

New
Growth
Press

www.newgrowthpress.com

New Growth Press, Greensboro, NC 27404
www.newgrowthpress.com
Copyright © 2012 by Susan Lutz.

All Scripture quotations, unless otherwise indicated, are taken
from the *Holy Bible, English Standard Version*® (ESV®), copyright © 2000, 2001 by Crossway Bibles, a division of Good News
Publishers. Used by permission. All rights reserved.

Scripture quotations marked NIV are taken from the *Holy Bible,
New International Version*®, NIV®. Copyright © 1973, 1978, 1984
by International Bible Society. Used by permission of Zondervan.
All rights reserved.

Cover Design: Faceout Books, faceout.com
Typesetting: Lisa Parnell, lparnell.com

ISBN 13: 978-1-938267-86-4
ISBN-13: 978-1-938267-11-6 (eBook)

Library of Congress Cataloging-in-Publication Data
Lutz, Susan, 1950–
  How do I look? : important questions in every girl's life / Susan Lutz.
    p. cm.
  Includes bibliographical references and index.
  ISBN-13: 978-1-938267-86-4 (alk. paper)
  1. Teenage girls—Religious life. 2. Christian teenagers—
Religious life. 3. Self-esteem in adolescence—Religious aspects—
Christianity. 4. Peer pressure in adolescence—Religious aspects—
Christianity. I. Title.
  BV4531.3.L88   2012
  248.8'33—dc23
                                                    2012026238

Printed in Canada

21 20 19 18 17 16 15 14   4 5 6 7 8

How do I look?

It's a simple question, right?

That depends on what you are really asking. Are you asking,

> Do my skinny jeans make me look fat?
> What do you think of my hair?
> Do you like this color on me?

We live in an image-obsessed world—with so many different ways to ask, How do I look? And so many different places to get answers. You can text, post, and tweet pictures of yourself 24/7. And you can follow your friends on Facebook, Tumblr, and Flickr from morning until night to see how they look too. And it's not just your friends. There are lots of celebrities to compare yourself to—TV, magazines, and websites are full of famous people who fit into size 2 skinny jeans (and some who don't!).

Of course you are comparing yourself, wondering whether you look good enough. And along with the questions and the doubts come other things—diets, laxatives, eating disorders, obsessive second-guessing about how you look and what you are wearing. You feel so much pressure because underneath the simple question, How do I look? are so many questions you don't usually say out loud, even to your best friend. Questions like:

> What do you really think about me?
> What do you say about me to our friends?

What does *he* think about me?
What does he say about me to *his* friends?
Do you like me?
Does *he* like me?
Do I fit in?
Am I okay or do I need to change somehow?

If you let yourself get quiet and *really* think about it, aren't those some of the questions you would *really* like the answers to? And, depending on the answers you get, aren't you also wondering, *Do I have a chance at being the person I'd like to be? Do I have a chance at being someone others will like?*

It's so odd, but just when you are trying to figure out who *you* are, suddenly it gets more and more important to know what others say about you. Those "underneath" questions are always lurking around in your head somewhere. And from middle school on, the answers you get matter so much. Your body is changing, your emotions are more on the surface, and you are much more aware of your future. It seems like everything is happening at once, and you're not quite sure how it's all going to turn out. You're not quite sure how *you* will turn out. No wonder it seems almost impossible to get a sense of who you are—your own identity— without some idea of how you come across to others. So even though you may be thinking more about yourself as an individual, there is no way that makes you independent. Instead, it is suddenly much more important to talk, dress, do your makeup, and choose activities and friends that will please the people whose opinions matter to you. It's a strange way to become yourself, isn't it? But in a certain sense, it's always been that way.

The First "How Do I Look?"

You can see it happening all the way back in the garden of Eden with Eve, the very first woman, and Adam, the first guy she laid eyes on. Eve's idea of who she was involved Adam's reaction to her. It started out pretty well—actually, incredibly easy. Eve didn't even have to ask the question. Adam took one look at her and was basically in awe. "At last! This is it!" he said (see Genesis 2:23). He responded to Eve with total acceptance, approval, delight—and maybe even relief after the time he'd spent without her. Adam was so happy with Eve—and she with him—that the Bible says, "[They] were both naked and were not ashamed" (Genesis 2:25). Isn't that the ultimate, perfect answer to the question, "How do I look?" The person you ask is so happy about who you are that you don't have to hide anything. And it's not just about your physical body. In the eyes of the other person, you have nothing to be ashamed of, inside or out. You are just right as you are. You can be yourself and enjoy it.

How many times have you felt that way? Is that a dream you left behind when you stopped watching *The Little Mermaid* and *Beauty and the Beast*? Is it what you are hoping for when you really fall in love?

It does sound almost too good to be true, doesn't it? And the reality is that this perfect moment didn't last. You probably know that it wasn't long before Eve and Adam decided to ignore God. They decided that to really be who they were meant to be, they needed to break away from God, go their own way, and make their own choices (Genesis 3:1–7). Now, the truth was that God had always given Adam and Eve lots of choices to make as people he had made in his image. There was a lot of freedom and purpose that went along with that. But when they decided not to trust God and to instead eat the fruit that he had told them not to, this was a choice that separated them from God. It turned out that being their own person *this* way shattered their relationship with God, the One who loved them most. They didn't see that until it was too late. But when they decided to go their own way and not God's way (what the Bible calls "sin"), they quickly discovered the damage they had done.

Going into Hiding

You might be wondering what all of this has to do with your life, but it turns out that what happened with God and Adam and Eve is the reason you have all those questions about yourself and others. Because once Adam and Eve broke their relationship with God, one of the first things that changed was their relationship with each other. The two changes went together. Before, because they were living as God intended and under his care, Adam and Eve had always been each other's safe place, each other's source of fun and companionship. But as soon as they ate the fruit, "the eyes of both were opened, and they knew that they were naked. And they sewed fig leaves together and made themselves loincloths" (Genesis 3:7).

Suddenly, they didn't want the other one to see them naked anymore. Now they had something to hide, something they felt guilty about, and the other one knew it. They didn't feel safe with that person anymore, and they couldn't go to God to fix it because they were hiding from him too (Genesis 3:8). Instead, they moved further away from each other. They blamed the other person for what had gone wrong instead of admitting their own part—just another way of hiding, really. They were no longer together as they once had been.

How many times have you felt this way? How much time do you spend hiding the things you don't like about yourself from people, hoping they won't see them and therefore will still accept you? Do you hide behind what you hope is the perfect hair and makeup? The clothes from the right stores? The newest phone? The right friends? Being good at sports or schoolwork? Going to the best parties?

Or does your hiding take you even further away from people? Are you retreating into your own private world by cutting? Or making yourself throw up? Or just not eating in the first place?

I admit it—it's a mess. Human beings were originally created to find themselves through their relationships, first with God and then with other people, but our broken relationship with God has made that much harder to do.

What Other People See—and Don't See

Does this mean you can't trust anyone anymore? No, but it means that when you want someone's approval to feel good about yourself, you have to remember a few things.

1. No one really has the ability to see, understand, love, and appreciate you the way Adam originally did Eve when they were living under God's protection. When they both were walking with God, neither one had anything to hide so there were no barriers between them.

2. When people look at you now, it's in a world where no one feels safe and secure the way they did before sin separated us from God. So when people look at you, it's not just about you anymore; it's also about them—how they see themselves, how you compare with them, and how you can help them or hurt them in getting what they think they need. (If you've thought about this at all, you probably realize that the same is true—at least some of the time!—for you too.)

3. Because of these changes, when you allow people to tell you who you are and what you are worth, you are giving them a power over you that they are most likely not wise enough or good enough to use well.

Giving Girls Power over You

Here is an example. In my high school class, one group of girls was at the top of the pile socially. Their social power was almost complete. They were the "mean girls" of our school. They controlled who went to the "best" parties, who got to be team captains or head cheerleader, who got elected to student government—you know the drill. If you had any questions about whether you were "in" or not, all you had to do was overstep your boundaries without their permission. Then you would find out.

What wasn't as obvious was that these girls were as hard on each other as they were on everyone else. Part of their routine was what they called lemon parties. They would gather for a sleepover at one girl's house and spend the night going over in great detail how each girl had to change if she wanted to stay in the group. Nothing was out of bounds—your hair, your teeth, your skin, your clothes, your activities, your grades, your friends, your dates—and nothing was negotiable. If you wanted to stay in the group, you had to make the change.

One night a girl I'll call Madison was told that she was too uptight. She had to loosen up and be more sexual with the boys the group hung out with. Madison was told that this was why she didn't have a boyfriend. At the next party Madison did what was expected of her so that everyone could see she had toed the line. It didn't matter if she wanted to or not. It mattered what the other girls had decided she needed to do.

How do you feel about that? Changing your nail polish because your friends don't like it is one thing. Giving away your sexuality—or smoking weed or dropping friends or cheating or doing something else destructive—because someone else tells you to is quite another. The girls in the group were the ones everyone else wanted to be. But there turned out to be a catch: those girls had to be who their *friends* wanted them to be. If they wanted everyone else's approval, even *they* couldn't be themselves.

Giving a Boy Power over You

Of course, you don't just let other girls define you—there are boys too. When I first met Emma, I thought she had everything going for her. She was pretty, great at sports, and always surrounded by friends. Emma was the life of the party, and everyone wanted to be where she was. But not everyone knew that Emma had an abusive relationship with Jake, a boy a few years older. For two years Jake spoiled every big occasion in Emma's life. She walked home crying after being crowned homecoming queen because of the way he treated her. She left the prom sobbing because of things he said and did. When I asked her why she stuck with him, she would only say, "I love him." But the truth was that she mostly loved being the girlfriend of the star of the football team. She admitted to me later, "I wanted to break up with him, but I didn't want to give up going out with him. I felt like people looked up to me because I was his girlfriend." Emma couldn't be herself or even enjoy her life because she was letting her relationship with Jake define her and tell her what she was worth. She was the girlfriend of the quarterback of the football team. That identity was more important to her than anything else.

Giving Others Power over You—
Is It Worth It?

I'm sure there were times when Madison and Emma wondered if it was worth it. But once you give others power over you, you get used to doing life that way. You get more and more dependent on other people's approval and less and less sure of yourself.

That's a problem when the other people are using the power you gave them to feel better about themselves, often at your expense.

Of course, they can't do it without your permission. You do have a choice once you see what's going on. One friend said to me, "I started out in high school looking for people's approval with my looks, my clothes, my boyfriends. When I entered the working world, I tried to get people's approval with things like my status, my income, and my professional success. After a while I realized that my 'rules' and standards for what would make me a worthwhile person kept changing as I got older. The things I was chasing didn't last from one season of my life to the next. But what never changed was that I always allowed other people to decide if

I was good enough or not. And I realized that was hurting me."

Another girl went down this road even further. Every time she met new people, she was so desperate for their approval that it was like they were voting on whether she was allowed to keep breathing or not. She got so anxious that she couldn't handle being around people, and the few she did trust were overwhelmed with her clinginess and neediness. Finally she realized, "I've treated other people like they were God. And I've assumed that God would treat me the same way other people did." She started looking for another way to do her life.

Another Way to Do Your Life

It can be depressing to talk about all this, especially since we usually spend our time telling ourselves that we can make it work. But really, there's got to be a better way to figure out who we are! And fortunately, there is. God is still here.

I realize that God may not be the first person you think of when you're looking for approval and self-acceptance. You might think, *God is* supposed *to love me. It doesn't count. And it's not going to make a difference for me at school.* Or, *I have no clue how to get in touch with him! This is way too much work over someone I can't see.* Or you might think, *How is it going to be easier to get God to approve of me when I can't even impress kids in my high school? That's* not *going to help!*

But take a step back and think about what happens when God isn't included in this part of your life. What happened when Adam and Eve walked away from him? Isn't that when all the fear and insecurity and hiding started? And what happens when *you* leave him on the sidelines? Ignoring him is what has given other people so much power in your life—power they don't deserve and often don't use well.

The truth is, we have always been meant to become who we really are through our relationship with God— the One who made us, who knows us best and loves us most. To leave him out is what makes you vulnerable to the weaknesses, betrayals, bad motives, and self-centeredness of everyone else. To start with him gives you a safe place, a secure place, a strong place to become the person you were always intended to be—even when the people you would normally count on let you down.

Molly's Story

Most of the time, our parents love us and want to encourage us as we grow up. Most of the time, we can see that even when we clash with them. But Molly had to learn to cope with a parent who hated her (and a lot of other people). A single mom, she blamed Molly for everything that was wrong in her life and threw her out of the house before she finished high school. Friends took her in so that she could finish her education and, considering everything she had been through, she was functioning pretty well . . . on the outside. But when it came to closer relationships, Molly tended to pick guys who didn't treat her much better than her mom and, not surprisingly, she had a hard time being able to give her heart to anyone. Inside, she was lost.

When we talked, we looked at promises God makes to his people, like Isaiah 49:15–16: "Can a mother forget the baby at her breast and have no compassion on the child she has borne? Though she may forget, I will not forget you! See, I have engraved you on the palms of my hands" (NIV). It became clear that Molly was burdened by the blame her mother had heaped upon her. Even though a part of her knew it was unfair, she still lived under its weight. She felt this was who she was. I said to her, "You have done things to feel guilty about, like all of us, but they are not the things your mom blames you for. You don't have to carry them. It's *not* who you are. And the things you *should* feel guilty about are things Jesus has already carried for you on the cross. You can bring those things to Jesus and receive his forgiveness and a new life to go along with it."

Over time, Molly came to understand that it was what God said about her that mattered. Her mother laid false guilt on her that she could not carry, but the Lord took her true guilt and paid the penalty himself. God adopted her as his child and gave her the love, acceptance, dignity, and security she had never received from her mother. This was not just an abstract "religious" idea to Molly. Because she believed it, it really was a new life for her.

Once Molly allowed God to tell her who she was and what she was worth, she had the strength to look at her relationship with her mother and consider what God might want her to do about it. She no longer lived under her mom's condemnation (though her mom hadn't changed), so she prayed and planned how she could show love to her mother without falling back into the toxic mess that was her mother's world. Since her mother would rarely answer the door when she stopped by, Molly left gifts on her porch for her birthday and Mother's Day. Occasionally, she would call and leave a friendly greeting on her mother's answering machine. A few years earlier, this would have just made Molly feel more and more angry, guilty, fearful, hopeless, and worthless. But now this wasn't the act of someone desperate for forgiveness and acceptance. It was the act of a person who knew she had *already* been forgiven, accepted, and loved by the Lord of the universe. *That* was who she was, loved by the God who had chosen to be her Father. And it was for that reason that she had something to share with an earthly mother who had nothing to give. Not long after that, Molly met a guy unlike anyone she had dated. She was able to love him and to receive his love. They married and now have three children.

When You Have Something to Hide

This was a story with a happy ending. But what if you are hiding from things about yourself that really *are* wrong? You can't face yourself, and you don't want anyone else to look at you either.

Jesus met a woman like that when he went to a village and stopped at the well to get a drink (John 4). It was midday and hot, so hardly anyone was there—just one woman. She was surprised to see Jesus. It seemed like she came at that time specifically to avoid running into anyone else. But as they talked, Jesus got past her prickly defensiveness and revealed her thirst for something to satisfy the ache in her heart. Toward the end of their conversation, Jesus said, "Go, call your husband, and come here" (4:16). "I have no husband," she replied. Then Jesus told her that he knew all about her past with its five husbands and her current, live-in lover. He then revealed himself as the God who is seeking people to love and worship him. In other words, he was inviting her to a relationship with him, just as she was. He saw all her junk and he still moved toward her.

What happened next? The woman hurried back to her village, to all the people she had been avoiding, and said, "Come, see a man who told me all that I ever did. Can this be the Christ?" (4:29). When she realized that Jesus saw her as she was, that he saw all that she was hiding, the burden she had been carrying suddenly fell away. When Jesus talked to her about her sin, it was a *relief* to her. He lifted her shame; he didn't increase it. He removed her burden as a foretaste of what he would eventually do for her when he died for her sins on the cross. And now the sin that had kept her isolated, ashamed, angry, defensive, lonely, and rejected no longer controlled her life. She was forgiven and her relationship with God was restored. She no longer had to hide from what other people said and thought about her. She let God define her, and she was free from the fear of rejection and free to love.

When It's Safe to Be Seen

Letting Jesus see who you are is the safest thing you could possibly do. At first that doesn't seem to make sense because he is perfectly holy, and you know your sin will be revealed. But when Jesus sees your sin, he offers to carry the burden of it and pay the penalty for it, so that all the choices that separated you from God can be cancelled and your relationship with him restored.

Are you weary of hiding so people will accept the person you *want* them to see? Are you looking for a way to be "naked and unashamed"—completely known, both good and bad, yet forgiven and accepted and loved by the One who sees it all but doesn't turn away? That's what it's like to give God the central place in your life, to get your life and value from him and let it open up the way you live.

God used a girl I will call Hilda Brandt to show me that this was what I needed. I was not in "the group" that ran things in my high school; I guess you could say I was on the "B" list and generally happy about it. In fact, we prided ourselves that we weren't as snobby and cutthroat as those other girls. But then Hilda Brandt came to our school after moving here from Germany. She was, to be honest, far from cute. She struggled with English. She wore a school uniform—the same one every day. She wore a hairnet like a lunch lady. The girls in my group of friends felt sorry for her and tried to be nice to her in class. But then she began sitting at our lunch table in the cafeteria without being invited. This meant that one of us always was displaced. Worse than that, it meant that we were seen by everyone else as Hilda's friends. This embarrassed and frustrated us. We didn't want people to connect us with her!

Not long after that, we noticed that during tests, Hilda had answers written in ink on her hands. Now, that was wrong, but what was also wrong was the way we used her cheating as an excuse to distance ourselves from her. The next time we went to lunch we all sat at a different table. Hilda had arrived first and was left to eat her lunch, all alone, at our regular table. We tried to tell ourselves that she deserved it—after all, she never asked if she could sit with us and she cheated on her tests!

But I was a Christian and I knew I was the one who had failed the test. I cared so much about what other people thought of me (including the other girls at my lunch table) that I ignored my conscience and purposely hurt a girl who was already hurting. I knew enough to feel sorry for someone whose looks and clothes and language and academics made it almost impossible for her to fit in. But when my reputation was threatened, I did not have it in me to love someone else more than myself. I cared more about what other people thought than what God thought, and I didn't even really want his help to do what was right and loving. In short, I was a mean girl too. Maybe my friends and I didn't have lemon parties, but I had my own things to be ashamed of, my own reasons to hide.

God showed me a couple of things through Hilda. First, the more I sought to get my identity and self-worth from other people, the more I would sacrifice my conscience and be far less than the person I was intended to be—and wanted to be. I was selling myself out, and it was a warped way to live! The second thing I learned was that even though God saw all my self-centeredness, insecurity, pride, and hard-heartedness, he didn't write me off. Instead, he forgave me because of Jesus' death on my behalf. He welcomed me back into relationship with him and gave me a heart that (gradually but genuinely) wanted to live the life he had for me. I found that the more I put the Lord first, the less I was afraid or intimidated by everyone else. And I also found that I could have healthy, unselfish relationships with others who had discovered the same thing.

God as Judge

The apostle Paul had to learn these lessons after he turned from persecuting Christians to becoming a follower of Christ himself. In 1 Corinthians 4:3–4 (NIV), he writes the following:

"I care very little if I am judged by you or by any human court." He had been freed from the trap of seeking everyone else's approval.

"Indeed, I do not even judge myself. My conscience is clear, but that does not make me innocent." This is the second trap. How many times, when people reject me, have I wanted to say, "But you don't understand! If you knew the real me, you wouldn't think of me that way. You wouldn't reject me." But that's not much of a refuge when you know that the real you is far from perfect. On top of that, it's just a way of trying to get yourself back into the *first* trap!

"It is the Lord who judges me." When I first read that sentence, I wanted to say, "Well, that's not much help. Being judged by God is not exactly a relaxing thought." But Paul knew what the woman at the well knew: when God shows you your sins, it is a relief because he invites you to lay them at his feet and receive his forgiveness. And from that point on he sees you as his child, with a great future ahead.

If you don't understand or believe what Jesus came to do for you, you won't be able to say what Paul said. But the last thing God wants you to do is to spend your life scrambling after the approval of other people, compromising your conscience and becoming less than you were created to be. God wants you to find your life in knowing, loving, and following him, the path intended for us all along. This is the way to a much bigger, fuller life that begins here and extends into forever! Don't let your life be consumed by whether you have the right shoes, the most awards, or the coolest friends. Dare to believe that God has something better, bolder, and more powerful, satisfying, and loving for you.

It starts with letting God tell you what he sees when he looks at you.

> But now thus says the LORD, he who created you, O Jacob, he who formed you, O Israel: "Fear not, for I have redeemed you; I have called you by name, you are mine. . . . you are precious in my eyes, and honored, and I love you. . . ." (Isaiah 43:1, 4)

> The LORD your God is in your midst, a mighty one who will save; he will rejoice over you with gladness; he will quiet you by his love; he will exult over you with loud singing. (Zephaniah 3:17)

> If God is for us, who can be against us? He who did not spare his own Son but gave him up for us all, how will he not also with him graciously give us all things? . . . For I am sure that neither death nor life, nor angels nor rulers, nor things present nor things to come, nor powers, nor height nor depth, nor anything else in all creation, will be able to separate us from the love of God in Christ Jesus our Lord. (Romans 8:31–32, 38–39)

> How great is the love the Father has lavished on
> us, that we should be called children of God!
> And that is what we are! (1 John 3:1 NIV)

Don't hide from God. Look into his face and let him show you what he sees. It is a lifelong process, but the more you come to know him, the more you will become yourself, and like the One who made you. Paul writes, "For now we see in a mirror dimly, but then face to face. Now I know in part; then I shall know fully, even as I have been fully known" (1 Corinthians 13:12).

How do I look? In the end you will say, "I look beautiful. I look loved. I look like my truest, best self. And I look like Jesus."

Talking It Over

1. What's your version of the question, "How do I look?"? What makes you feel good about yourself? What makes you feel secure?

2. Have you ever had a relationship where you felt completely understood and accepted for who you are? What made it that way?

3. What was wrong with the way Adam and Eve tried to be themselves? What unintended consequences did this choice have?

4. Do you have any "mean girl" experiences? Have you ever had a "Jake" in your life? When did you realize what he or she was doing, and how did you get out?

5. What might be a good reason to allow God to help you with the way you see yourself? What might you gain? How might you be protected?

6. What's the difference between the false guilt other people might place on you and the true guilt God talks to us about?

7. How did God's view of Molly make a difference to her? What did it enable her to do? How did it protect her and free her up?

8. When Jesus met the woman at the well, how did he show her it was safe to be seen by him? Does this make you look at Jesus differently? Does it make you look at your sin differently? Does it mean our sins don't really matter?

9. How does 1 Corinthians 4:3–4 change the way you think about the approval of others?

10. How do you look to God? Why? How does that change the way you look at yourself?

Simple, Quick, Biblical

Advice on Complicated Counseling Issues for Pastors, Counselors, and Individuals

MINIBOOK
CATEGORIES

- Personal Change
- Marriage & Parenting
- Medical & Psychiatric Issues
- Women's Issues
- Singles
- Military

USE YOURSELF | GIVE TO A FRIEND | DISPLAY IN YOUR CHURCH OR MINISTRY

New Growth Press

Go to **www.newgrowthpress.com** or call **336.378.7775** to purchase individual minibooks or the entire collection. Durable acrylic display stands are also available to house the minibook collection.